MY FAVORITE TOYS

by Pearl Markovics

Consultant:
Beth Gambro
Reading Specialist
Yorkville, Illinois

Contents

My Favorite Toys............2

Key Words 16

Index.....................16

About the Author 16

Bearport
PUBLISHING

New York, New York

My Favorite Toys

What do you love?

I love toys!

I love kites.

Look at them fly.

I love balls.

Look at them bounce.

I love tops.

Look at them spin.

I love bikes.

Look at them race.

I love robots.

Look at them walk.

Pick your favorite!

What toy do you love?

15

Key Words

balls

bikes

kites

robots

tops

Index

balls 6–7   kites 4–5   tops 8–9
bikes 10–11 robots 12–13

About the Author

Pearl Markovics has many favorite things. She collects very tiny toys.